My Pinkie Finger

**Written by
Betsy Franco**

**Illustrated by
Margeaux Lucas**

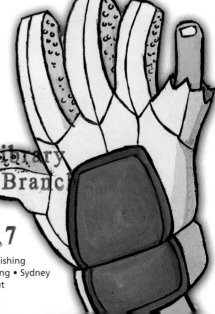

**℗
Children's Press®**
A Division of Grolier Publishing
New York • London • Hong Kong • Sydney
Danbury, Connecticut

For Davy
—B. F.

To my beloved brothers, Jim and John
—M. L.

Reading Consultant
Katharine A. Kane
Education Consultant
(Retired, San Diego County Office of Education
and San Diego State University)

Visit Children's Press® on the Internet at:
http://publishing.grolier.com

Library of Congress Cataloging-in-Publication Data
Franco, Betsy.
  My pinkie finger / by Betsy Franco ; illustrated by Margeaux Lucas.
    p. cm. — (Rookie reader)
  Summary: A child describes some of the ways that show how much he
has grown.
  ISBN 0-516-22221-X (lib. bdg.)   0-516-27295-0 (pbk.)
  [1. Growth—Fiction. 2. Stories in rhyme.] I. Lucas, Margeaux, ill.
II. Title. III. Series.
PZ8.3.F84765 My 2001
[E]—dc21   00-029530

GROLIER
PUBLISHING
3 4 5 6 7 8 9 10 R 10 09 08 07 06 05 04

My pinkie finger is longer
than it ever used to be.

3

I've grown so much,
my grandma says
she hardly knows it's me.

5

My pants are short.

My coat is small.

Next to my sister, I look so tall!

With long, strong legs,

how high I go.

I'm extra tall on tippy-toe.

I leap way up to catch a ball.

Come see! I'm walking on a wall.

I'm keeping track.

I grow and grow.

How big I'll get, I do not know.

My pinkie finger is longer
than it ever used to be.

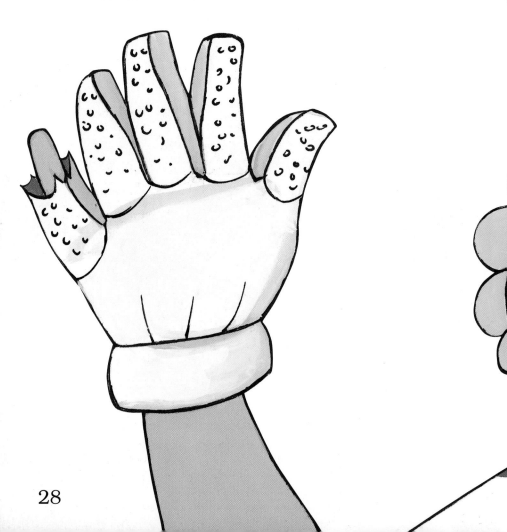

When Grandpa comes,
he's so surprised.
I have to say, "It's me!"

Word List (70 words)

a	go	it	on	tippy-toe
and	grandma	it's	pants	to
are	Grandpa	keeping	pinkie	track
ball	grow	know	say	up
be	grown	knows	says	used
big	hardly	leap	see	walking
catch	have	legs	she	wall
coat	he's	long	short	way
come	high	longer	sister	when
comes	how	look	small	with
do	I	me	so	
ever	I'll	much	strong	
extra	I'm	my	surprised	
finger	I've	next	tall	
get	is	not	than	

About the Author

Betsy Franco lives in Palo Alto, California, where she has written more than forty books for children—picture books, poetry, and nonfiction. Many of her ideas come from the funny things her children said when they were young. Betsy is the only female in her family, which includes her husband Douglas, her three sons, and Lincoln the cat. She starts writing in the wee hours of the morning when everyone but Lincoln is asleep.

About the Illustrator

Margeaux Lucas has been illustrating children's books for five years. She lives in Brooklyn, New York, with piles of paper, hundreds of pencils, countless tubes of paint, and a spotted cat named Flump.